To Christine

Wonderful to be amongst the Premantles.
Thank you so much for coming up to
Scapa.

June 2019

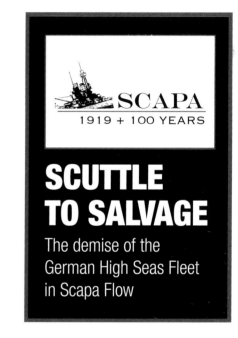

SCAPA
1919 + 100 YEARS

SCUTTLE TO SALVAGE

The demise of the
German High Seas Fleet
in Scapa Flow

NICHOLAS JELLICOE

Published by The Orcadian (Kirkwall Press)
Hell's Half Acre, Kirkwall, Orkney, KW15 1GJ
Tel.: 01856 879000 • Fax.: 01856 879001

www.orcadian.co.uk

Book sales: www.orcadian.co.uk/shop/index.php

ISBN No. 978-1-912889-03-7

Printed in Orkney by The Orcadian, Hatston Print Centre,
Hell's Half Acre, Kirkwall, Orkney, Scotland, KW15 1GJ

SCAPA
1919 + 100 YEARS

To the memory of those German sailors who never made it home.

THE GREAT SCUTTLE

On a midsummer's day in 1919, fifty German ships displacing more than 430,000 tons were sunk by their crews in Scapa Flow, Orkney. They were part of the 74 ships of the German High Seas Fleet, interned there during the peace negotiations in Paris which had started after the armistice of 11 November 1919 had brought the First World War on the Western Front to a halt.

It was the biggest single loss of shipping in history.

The ships had ended up in the Flow after often acrimonious discussion amongst the Allied victors. The British did not want any of the ships to be given to the French Navy as compensation for France's war losses; the Americans had wanted the ships destroyed rather than passed to Great Britain.

DIE SELBSVERSENKUNG DER DEUTSCHE FLOTTE

Am Mittsommertag 1919 wurden fünfzig deutsche Schiffe mit einer Gesamttonnage von mehr als 430.000 Tonnen von ihren Besatzungen in Scapa Flow, Orkney, versenkt. Sie gehörten zu den 74 Schiffen der deutschen Hochseeflotte, die dort während der Friedensverhandlungen in Paris interniert waren, nachdem der Waffenstillstand vom 11. November 1919 den Ersten Weltkrieg an der Westfront zum Erliegen gebracht hatte.

Es war der größte Einzelverlust der Schifffahrtsgeschichte.

Die Schiffe waren, nach oft erbitterten Diskussionen, unter den alliierten Siegern im Flow gelandet. Die Briten wollten nicht, dass eines der Schiffe an die französische Marine übergeben wurde, um die Kriegsverluste Frankreichs auszugleichen. Die Amerikaner wollten, dass die Schiffe zerstört werden, anstatt in britische Hände zu gelangen.

SCAPA
1919 + 100 YEARS

MUTINY IN THE GERMAN FLEET

Since war's outbreak in August 1914, only a small political opposition existed in Germany. As the war continued, the first signs of trouble appeared in the High Seas Fleet in summer 1917. Then it was about bad food and poor leadership, but the socialist peace conference in Stockholm also played a catalytic role. Then stokers walked off the *Prinzregent Luitpold* when a film was cancelled. It escalated and on 1 August, more than 400 sailors went ashore in Wilhelmshaven to demonstrate. Two sailors, 23-year-old Max Reichpietsch and the 25-year-old Albin Köbis, were identified as ringleaders and executed by firing squad.

While the High Seas Fleet remained mostly inactive during the war due to the British Blockade, with peace in sight the Navy command developed a plan for a last sortie. It was an effort to save its honour by underlining its willingness to contribute to the war untill the very end. For many sailors, this was the last straw: from their point of view their officers were acting against the country's government's efforts to end the war. Many sailors refused orders. Mutiny spread from ship to ship and soon crews started to leave the battle-cruisers, *Derfflinger* and *Seydlitz.*

Under orders from the fleet commander, von Hipper, torpedo boats and a submarine threated the battleships *Thüringen* and *Helgoland* which were both under the control of the mutineers. The ships went back to Wilhelmshaven, the fleet action was cancelled and the mutineers were arrested. When a squadron was moved to Kiel in an effort to calm the situation, the unrest changed from mutiny to revolution, as strike-experienced workers began to support the sailors' movement. From Kiel, what started as a mutiny now spread as revolution throughout Germany.

MEURTEREI IN DER DEUTSCHER FLOTTE

Zu Kriegsbeginn gab es im Deutschen Reich nur eine kleine Opposition gegen den Krieg. Doch mit fortschreitendem Krieg wuchs sie an und erreichte einen ersten Höhepunkt im Sommer 1917. Schlechte Ernährung und das Empfinden ungerechter Behandlung waren die Hauptursachen, aber auch die internationale sozialistische Friedenskonferenz in Stockholm spielte eine Katalysatorrolle. Heizer von SMS *Prinzregent Luitpold* verließen nach einer abgesagten Filmvorführung eigenmächtig das Schiff. Die Situation eskalierte und am 1. August gingen mehr als 400 Matrosen in Wilhelmshaven an Land, um zu demonstrieren. Zwei Matrosen, der 23-jährige Max Reichpietsch und der 25-jährige Albin Köbis, wurden als Anführer identifiziert und von einem Erschießungskommando exekutiert.

Während die Hochseeflotte aufgrund der britischen Blockade weitgehend inaktiv gewesen war, entwickelte die Seekriegsleitung einen Plan für einen letzten Einsatz: er sollte die Kampfbereitschaft bis zum Ende unterstreichen und die Ehre der Flotte bewahren. Für viele Matrosen brachte dies das Fass zum Überlaufen: in ihren Augen diente der Plan der Offiziere dazu, die Friedensverhandlung der Regierung zu untergraben. Etliche Matrosen verweigerten den Gehorsam. Nun breitete sich die Meuterei von Schiff zu Schiff aus, und schon bald begannen die Mannschaften, die Schlachtkreuzer SMS Derfflinger und Seydlitz zu verlassen.

Auf Befehl des Befehlshabers der Hochseeflotte, von Hipper, zwangen Torpedoboote und ein U-Kreuzer die in der Hand der Meuterer befindlichen Großkampfschiffe Thüringen und Helgoland durch Anrdohung von Waffengewalt zur Aufgabe. Die Schiffe liefen zurück nach Wilhelmshaven, der Flottenvorstoß wurde abgebrochen und die Meuterer inhaftiert. Als ein Geschwader zur Beruhigung der Situation nach Kiel verlegte, wandelte sich der Aufstand von einer Meuterei zur Revolution, nachdem streikerfahrene Arbeiter begonnen hatten, die Proteste der Matrosen zu unterstützen. Von Kiel aus breitete sich die Protestbewegung als Revolution über das gesamte Reichsgebiet aus.

SCAPA
1919 + 100 YEARS

Max Reichpietsch, Schiff Friedrich der Große. Erschossen am 7. Sept. 1917.

Albin Köbes, Schiff Prinzregent Luitpold. Erschossen am 7. Sept. 1917.

Sie wirkten als Sozialisten unter ihren Kameraden und fielen als Opfer des Tirpitz-Geistes.

1. Unrest in the summer of 1917 led to sailors leaving their ships. Two sailors, Max Reichpietsch and Albin Köbis, were named as ringleaders and executed by firing squad.

---

1. *Unruhen im Sommer 1917 führten dazu, dass Matrosen ihre Schiffe verließen. Zwei Matrosen, Max Reichpietsch und Albin Köbis, wurden als Rädelsführer verurteilt und von einem Erschießungskommando hingerichtet.*

Die sich in See zu gehen weigernde Mannschaft S. „Thüringen" wird von U-Kreuzer und Torpedobooten zur Kapitulation gezwungen.
→ X U-Kreuzer

2. SMS *Thüringen* at anchor close to Wilhelmshaven at the end of October 1918. U.135 can be seen on her starboard beam in this re-enactment. Following Admiral Hipper's (**3**) orders she (and the torpedoboats) were to fire upon mutineers on board.

2. *SMS Thüringen Ende Oktober 1918 vor Anker in der Nähe von Wilhelmshaven. In dieser Nachstellung ist U.135 an ihrer Steuerbordseite zu sehen. Auf Befehl von Admiral Hipper (3) sollten sie (und die Torpedoboote) notfalls auf die Meuterer an Bord der SMS Thüringen schießen.*

4. The Social Democrat, Gustav Noske addressing returning submariners (5) in Kiel, November 1918 in the hope of calming the situation.

4. *Der Sozialdemokrat (SPD) Gustav Noske sprach im November 1918 zu den zurückkehrenden U-Boot Matrosen (5) in Kiel in der Hoffnung, die Situation zu beruhigen.*

6. German revolutionary sailors of the Soldiers' Council gather for a group photo on board SMS *Prinzregent Luitpold*. 7. Sailors marching into Wilhelmshaven to protest.

8. Mutinous sailors marching out of their barracks, Wilhelmshaven November 1918. 9. The sailors' demands being announced 6 November. 10. Mass rally 10 November. 11. Meeting of the Soldiers' Council 11 November.

6. Revolutionäre Matrosen des Soldatenrats treffen sich an Bord von SMS Prinzregent Luitpold für ein Gruppenfoto. 7. Matrosen marschieren aus Protest nach Wilhelmshaven.

8. Meuternde Matrosen marschieren aus ihrer Kaserne, Wilhelmshaven, November 1918. 9. Die Forderungen der Matrosen werden am 6. November verkündet. 10. Massenkundgebung am 10. November. Marinemeuterei. 11. Sitzung des Soldatenrates am 11. November.

...lligung der Forderungen
...der Marinesoldaten
...en Chef der Marinestation der Nor...
— Wilhelmshaven, ... —
phot. W.Sch.

Ansprache des SOLDATENRAT's
an die Menge bei der grosen
Demonstration am 10. 11. 18 W'haven.

12. Revolutionary insignia : an armband and a defaced Cap tally from SMS *Braunswchweig*. **13.** *Helgoland* sailor, Carl Linke's diaries, document his growing disillusionment with the war. **14.** Theodore Plivier's novel, *The Kaiser's Coolies*, became a classic describing conditions in the fleet. **15.** Stoker Bernhard Kuhnt declared himself first President of the new republic of Oldenburg.

16. The Wilhelmshaven Soldiers' and Sailors' Revolutionary Committee (The Council of 21) includes the revolutionaries Bernhard Kuhnt and Kurt Albers.

12. Revolutionäre Abzeichen: Eine Armbinde und ein entstelltes Mützenband von SMS Braunschweig 13. Die Tagebücher des Matrosen Carl Richard Linke dokumentieren seine wachsende Enttäuschung während des Krieges. 14. Theodore Plieviers Roman des Kaiser's Kulis wurde zu einem Klassiker, der die Bedingungen in der Hochseeflotte beschreibt. 15. Heizer Bernhard Kuhnt erklärte sich zum ersten Präsidenten der neuen Republik Oldenburg.

16. Zum als 21er Rat bezeichneten Revolutionskomittee von Wilhelmshaven gehören die Revolutionäre Bernhard Kuhnt und Kurt Albers.

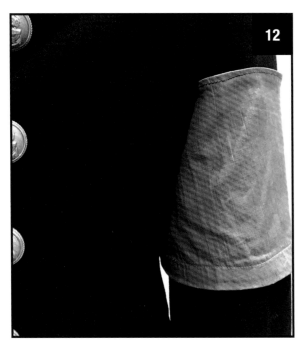

Der 21er Rat des Arbeiter- und Soldaten-Rates der Nordseestation

Hartung   Henneicke   Bruster   Ramsauer   Handschuch

Dorn   Imhoff   Hehne   Unruh   Siekmann   Waldau   Wengora   Driesen   Winter

     Druschke   Zimmermann   Bartels   Albers   Kuhnt   Schmitz   Pflug   Schneider   Höch

17. Guarding the barracks after fellow German sailors have been released from prison, Wilhelmshaven. 18. The revolution spreads to Berlin. 19. Street-fighting in Berlin.

20. Street-fighting in Berlin.

17. Kasernenwachen in Wilhelmshaven nach der Befreiung inhaftierter Kameraden. 18. Revolution in Berlin. 19. Strassenkampf in Berlin.

20. Strassenkampf in Berlin.

1

21. The 1958 East German film *Das Lied der Matrosen* (The Sailor's Song) glorified the Naval Mutiny.

22. Red flags and the deletion to the reference of His Majesty's ship is shown on a contemporary postcard of *König Albert*.

---

21. *Der in der DDR produzierte Film „Das Lied der Matrosen" aus dem Jahr 1958 verherrlichte die Meuterei.*

22. *Auf einer zeitgenössischen Postkarte von SMS König Albert sind rote Flaggen und die Streichung der Buchstaben "SM" (="Seiner Majestät") aus dem Kürzel SMS, das für "Seiner Majestät Schiff" steht, zu sehen.*

S. „König Albert".

MILITARY COLLAPSE AND THE GERMAN REVOLUTION

The last shots of the First World War were fired on the Western Front. On the morning of 11 November 1918, at eleven o'clock, the guns went silent. It was a moment of jubilation for the allies, profound demoralisation for Germany but relief for all. After four years and the deaths of 20 million, the war was finally over.

Deep in the forests of France at Compiègne, the political and military representatives of the belligerent nations handed over the terms of a ceasefire in a train carriage. On another train, following his abdication, the ex-Kaiser of Germany took his family into exile, opening up a new moment in German history.

Germany's Navy, however, technically undefeated in battle (as they had, for the most part remained in harbour) and, though a fleet in the throes of mutiny and dissent, still represented a credible armed threat. Integral to the armistice process, then, was the decision to intern a large number of German ships as a guarantor that the peace negotiations would be carried out in good faith.

23. The railway car at Compiègne with the representatives of the allies. Among others, at the meeting were Admirals Wemyss and Hope (left), in front of them is German Secretary of State Matthias Erzberger. Standing at the table is General Foch beside whom sits General Weygand.

23. *Der Eisenbahnwagen in Compiègne mit den Vertretern der Alliierten. An dem Treffen nahmen unter anderem Admirals Wemyss und Hope (links) teil, vor ihnen der deutsche Außenminister Matthias Erzberger. Am Tisch steht General Foch, neben ihm sitzt General Weygand.*

DER MILITÄRISCHE ZUSAMMENBRUCH UND DIE DEUTSCHE REVOLUTION

Die letzten Schüsse des Ersten Weltkriegs wurden an der Westfront abgefeuert. Am Morgen des 11. November 1918 um elf Uhr verstummten die Geschütze. Es war ein Moment des Jubels für die Allierten, eine tief greifende Demoralisierung für Deutschland, aber Erleichterung für alle. Nach vier Jahren und dem Tod von 20 Millionen Menschen war der Krieg endlich vorbei.

Tief in den Wäldern Frankreichs in Compiègne hatten die politischen und militärischen Vertreter der kriegführenden Nationen einen Waffenstillstand in einem Eisenbahnwaggon unterzeichnet. In einem anderen Zug brachte der ehemalige Deutsche Kaiser seine Familie ins Exil und eröffnete damit ein neues Kapitel in der deutschen Geschichte.

Die deutsche Marine, formal in der Schlacht unbesiegt (da die Schlachtflotte, zum Großteil des Krieges, zur Untätigkeit gezwungen) stellte trotz der Meuterei und ihrer inneren Zerrissenheit immer noch eine glaubwürdige bewaffnete Bedrohung dar. Ein wesentlicher Bestandteil der Waffenstillstandsverhandlungen war daher die Entscheidung, eine große Anzahl deutscher Schiffe zu internieren, um sicherzustellen, dass die Friedensverhandlungen ungestört durchgeführt werden konnten.

SCAPA
1919 + 100 YEARS

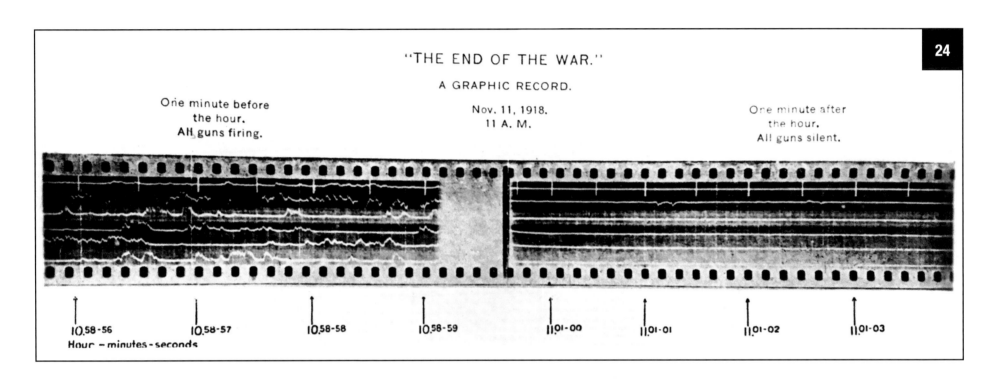

"THE END OF THE WAR."

A GRAPHIC RECORD.

One minute before
the hour.
All guns firing.

Nov. 11, 1918.
11 A. M.

One minute after
the hour.
All guns silent.

10.58-56   10.58-57   10.58-58   10.58-59   11.01-00   11.01-01   11.01-02   11.01-03

Hour – minutes - seconds

24. An artillery sound recording before and after the armistice came into effect at 11:00 on 11 November 1918.

25. The Kaiser in exile in the Netherlands following his abdication on 9 November 1918. **26.** The Kaiser at Doorn with his second wife (Prinzessin Hermine von Schönaich-Carolath) and step-daughter (Henriette), March 1931.

24. Eine Tonaufnahme der Artillerie vor und nach dem Waffenstillstand, der am 11. November 1918 um 11:00 Uhr in Kraft trat.

25. Der Kaiser im Exil in den Niederlanden nach seiner Abdankung am 9. November 1918. 26. Der ex-Kaiser mit seiner zweiten Frau (Prinzessin Hermine von Schönaich-Carolath) und Stieftochter (Henriette) im niederländischen Doorn, März 1931.

F.Finke
Wilhelmshaven

Engl. Luftschiff geleitet die deutschen Torpedoboote
nach Scapa Flow

THE HIGH SEAS FLEET'S LAST JOURNEY

Days after the armistice was signed, Admiral Sir David Beatty met with German naval representatives on his flagship, HMS *Queen Elizabeth*. At midnight on November 16, Rear Admiral von Meurer, the German representative left for Kiel with his orders. The High Seas Fleet was to be delivered into allied hands in Scotland's east coast naval base, Rosyth five days later.

The allies demanded 74 ships. Crews frantically removed anything that could assist in the hostile use of the ships – torpedoes, munitions, firing mechanisms. Coal, water and provisions were loaded up for an anticipated 37-day internment.

Under the command of Rear Admiral Ludwig von Reuter, the man chosen by the Commander in Chief, Admiral Hipper to take these once proud ships into captivity, the great procession left home harbours.

They were met by more than 250 heavily armed allied ships. Cheering British sailors kept each ship under its guns, manning their guns and torpedo tubes. At sunset, Beatty announced that the German flag was to be hauled down and not to be raised again until he allowed it.

27. The German fleet crossing the North Sea with a British airship escort.

DER LETZTE REISE DER HOCHSEEFLOTTE

Tage nach der Unterzeichnung des Waffenstillstands, traf Admiral Sir David Beatty auf seinem Flaggschiff, der HMS Queen Elizabeth, mit deutschen Marinevertretern zusammen. Am 16. November um Mitternacht reiste der deutsche Vertreter, Vizeadmiral von Meurer, zur Befehlsausgabe nach Kiel. Die Hochseeflotte sollte fünf Tage später in Rosyth, einer Marinebasis an Schottlands Ostküste, den Alliierten übergeben werden.

74 Schiffe wurden von den Alliierten gefordert. Die Besatzungen entfernten hektisch alles, was für Feindseligkeiten hätte genutzt werden können - Torpedos, Munition und Zündmechanismen. Kohle, Wasser und Vorräte wurden für eine voraussichtliche 37-tägige Internierung gebunkert.

Unter dem Kommando von Konteradmiral Ludwig von Reuter, ausgewählt von Oberbefehlshaber Admiral Hipper, um diese einst stolzen Schiffe in Gefangenschaft zu bringen, verließ der Verband seinen Heimathafen.

Er wurde von mehr als 250 schwer bewaffneten Schiffen der Alliierten empfangen. Jubelnde britische Matrosen behielten jedes Schiff im Visier und besetzten deren Geschütze und Torpedorohre. Am Ende des Tages kündigte Beatty an, dass die deutsche Fahne einzuholen war, und erst nach seiner Erlaubnis wieder gehisst werden dürfe.

27. Die deutsche Flotte überquert die Nordsee mit einer britischen Luftschiffeskorte.

SCAPA
1919 + 100 YEARS

28. Rear Admiral Hugo von Meurer was sent by Hipper to meet with Admiral Sir David Beatty and his staff to organise the Internment planning aboard HMS *Queen Elizabeth* (**29**). There was little British compromise to German requests.

28. *Konteradmiral Hugo von Meurer wurde von Hipper zu einem Treffen mit Admiral Sir David Beatty und seinen Stab geschickt, um die Planung der Internierung an Bord der HMS Queen Elizabeth (**29**) zu organisieren. Deutschen Anliegen gegenüber zeigten die Briten wenig Kompromissbereitschaft.*

30. The Allied Naval Commission regularly visited Wilhelmshaven to inspect German ships before and after the fleet left. **31.** The crew of the light cruiser *Regensburg* waiting for their arrival.

30. *Die Alliierte Marinekommission besuchte regelmäßig Wilhelmshaven, um deutsche Schiffe vor und nach dem Auslaufen der Flotte zu inspizieren.* **31.** *Die Besatzung des leichten Kreuzers Regensburg wartet auf die Ankunft der Marinekommission.*

32. Ammunition being unloaded from *Prinzregent Luitpold* (or *König Albert*). **33.** Unloading munitions from the High Seas Fleet flagship, *Friedrich der Große* in Wilhelmshaven. Any valuable technology, like range-finding equipment, was offloaded. **34.** The last Sunday. Crews aboard ship in home harbour, Wilhelmshaven. 17 November 1918.

32. *Munition wird von Prinzregent Luitpold (oder König Albert) abgeladen.* **33.** *Abmunitionierung des Flaggschiffs der Hochseeflotte, Friedrich der Große, in Wilhelmshaven. Alle wertvollen Technologien, wie zum Beispiel Entfernungsmesser, wurden von Bord genommen.* **34.** *Der letzte Sonntag in der Heimat. Besatzungen an Bord eines Schiffes in, Wilhelmshaven am 17. November 1918.*

Fot. Strohschein.
.145.

Letzter Sonntag vor der Internierung
in Wilhelmshaven, am 17. Nov. 1918.

35 (in image)

S. „Derfflinger"s Ausfahrt zur Internierung am 17. November 1918 aus Wilhelmshaven
Phot. Strohschein 147

36. While most of Germany's surface fleet was interned, the submarine forces were surrendered and most sunk. *UB.99* (shown below) became part of the French Navy.

36. *Während der größte Teil der deutschen Überwasserstreitkräfte interniert wurde, wurden die U-Boot-Verbände ausgeliefert und die meisten versenkt. UB.99 (hier abgebildet) wurde von der französischen Marine übernommen.*

36 (in image)

35. The battle-cruiser *Derfflinger* leaving Wilhelmshaven harbour 17 November 1918.

35. *Der Schlachtkreuzer Derfflinger verlässt Wilhelmshaven am 17. November 1918.*

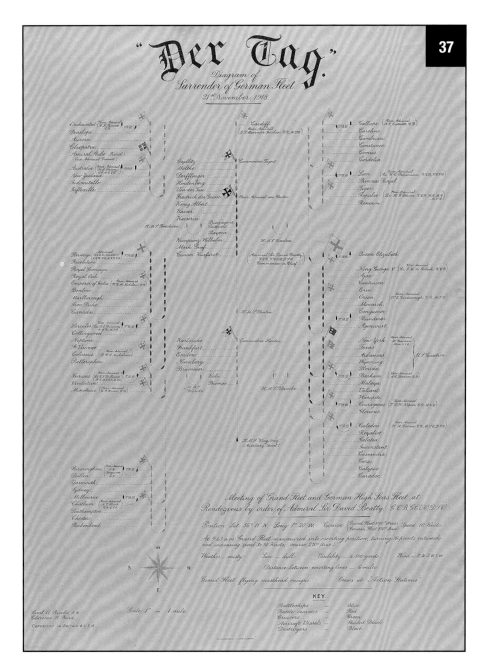

37. A British commemorative print showing the escort formation on 21 November 1918. **38.** SMS *Kaiser* steams into internment past the destroyer put aside for photographers.

37. *Ein britisches Gedenkblatt zeigt die Verbände, die am 21. November 1918 die deutschen Einheiten empfingen.* **38.** *SMS Kaiser auf dem Weg in die Internierung, dampft an einem für Fotografen reservierten Zerstörer vorbei.*

39. Admiral Sir David Beatty, C-in-C of the Grand Fleet, takes the salute. **40.** A view of Beatty's flagship, HMS *Queen Elizabeth*, from the deck of an American battleship of the 6th Battle Squadron at Cromarty, in the Firth of Forth. **41.** British sailors wearing anti-flash protection in the turrets watch the German ships arrive. No risks were taken lest there might be an incident that sparked renewed hostilities.

39. *Admiral Sir David Beatty, Befehlshaber der Grand Fleet, nimmt den Gruß entgegen.* **40.** *Ein Blick auf sein Flaggschiff, HMS Queen Elizabeth, aufgenommen vom Deck eines amerikanischen Linieschiffes der 6. Battle Squadron in Cromarty, Firth of Forth.* **41.** *Britische Matrosen in Türmen mit Flammenschutzanzügen beobachten die Ankunft der deutschen Schiffe. Man war für die Evantualität erneuter Feindseligkeiten gerüstet.*

42. SMS *Emden*, *Frankfurt* and *Bremse* arrive in Scapa Flow, 24 November 1918. **43.** The commanders under whose authority the Internment would be managed: Admiral Sir Charles Madden, C-in-C Atlantic fleet**. 44.** Vice Admiral Sir Sydney Fremantle, C-in-C 1st Battle Squadron, Atlantic fleet. **45.** Rear Admiral Ludwig von Reuter, C-in-C Interned German fleet. **46.** Admiral von Trotha, head of the German Admiralty.

42. *Die Kleinen Kreuzer SMS Emden, Frankfurt und Bremse treffen am 24. November 1918 in Scapa Flow ein.* **43.** *Die für die Internierung verantwortlichen Kommandeure: Admiral Sir Charles Madden, Befehlshaber der Britishen Atlantikflotte.* **44.** *Vizeadmiral Sir Sydney Fremantle, Befehlshaber des I. Schlachtgeschwaders der Britishen Atlantikflotte.* **45.** *Konteradmiral Ludwig von Reuter, Befehlshaber der internierten Deutsche Flotte in Scapa Flow.* **46.** *Admiral von Trotha, Chef des Marinekabinetts.*

LIFE ON THE FLOW

Only after leaving Rosyth did Rear Admiral von Reuter discover the Internment fleet's final destination: Scapa Flow in the islands of Orkney. Internment would be more like imprisonment as sailors were not allowed off their own ships, let alone go ashore. Only Reuter and the fleet chaplains could do that, provided they had permission and only under guard.

With the fleet came 20,000 German naval officers and men but, after Reuter had sent the most unreliable elements and revolutionaries back to Germany, only a skeleton crew of 1,800 of the most reliable remained.

At a high price, only fresh water and coal was provided by the British. Food, drink and everyday living necessities were delivered directly from Germany. Diets were supplemented by using engine oil to fry the plentiful local fish caught in torpedo nets, shooting seagulls with crossbows or Verey pistols or catching members of the unwelcome rat population. Sailors with severe dental problems would have to await their return to Germany as no dentist was available. It was even rumoured that there had been night time raids in which sheep were stolen even though this was a potentially life-threatening escapade. Naturally, though, there was a thriving black market, of which few talk about to this day. Toothpaste could be exchanged for a coveted medal, the Iron Cross.

Activities were, as in most prison camp routines, repetitive and increasingly mundane and sports on the shorter destroyer decks was, at best, difficult. The men occupied themselves by playing music and educating themselves, filling the endless hours with the smallest activity.

47. Sailors on the former flagship, SMS *Friedrich der Große*.

47. *Matrosen auf dem ehemaligen Flaggschiff SMS Friedrich der Große.*

LEBEN AUF SCAPA FLOW

Erst als er Rosyth verlassen hatte, erhielt von Reuter Kenntnis vom endgültigen Ziel der Flotte: Scapa Flow auf den Orkney-Inseln. Die Internierung glich eher einer Kriegsgefangenschaft. Die Matrosen durften ihre Schiffe nicht verlassen, geschweige denn an Land gehen. Dies durften nur von Reuter und die Kapläne. Auch sie bedurften hierzu einer Erlaubnis und wurden währenddessen bewacht.

Der Internierungsverband zählte zunächst 20.000 deutsche Marineoffiziere und Mannschaften, aber nachdem Reuter die unzuverlässigsten Personen und Revolutionäre nach Deutschland zurückgeschickt hatte, verblieben nur 1800 der Zuverlässigsten als Rumpfbesatzung in Scapa Flow.

Trinkwasser und Kohle wurden von den Briten zu einem hohen Preis geliefert. Lebensmittel, Getränke und Alltagsbedarf wurden direkt aus Deutschland geliefert. Die Mahlzeiten wurden durch in Maschinenöl gebratenen einheimischen Fisch ergänzt. Dieser war reichlich vorhanden und wurde mit Torpedofangnetzen gefangen. Möwen wurden mit Armbrüsten oder Verey-Pistolen geschossen. Auch die zahlreichen missliebigen Ratten wurden als Nahrung gefangen und verzehrt. Seeleute mit schweren Zahnproblemen müssten auf ihre Rückkehr nach Deutschland warten, da kein Zahnarzt zur Verfügung stand. Es wurde sogar gemunkelt, dass es nachts überfälle an Land gab um Schafe zu stehlen, obwohl diese Eskapaden potentiell lebensgefährlich waren.

Natürlich gab es einen florierenden Schwarzmarkt, aber bis heute reden nur wenige darüber. Zahnpasta konnte gegen eine begehrte Medaille, das Eiserne Kreuz, eingetauscht werden.

Die Aktivitäten waren, wie in den meisten Gefangenenlagern, eintönig und zunehmend banal, und Sport auf den kürzeren Zerstörerdecks war bestenfalls schwierig. Die Männer beschäftigten sich mit Musik, ihrer Ausbildung und füllten die endlosen Stunden mit der kleinsten Aktivität.

48

49. Battleship, SMS *Bayern* in Scapa Flow with SMS *Emden* in the background.

49. *Schlachtschiff SMS Bayern in Scapa Flow mit SMS Emden im Hintergrund.*

48. From March 1919, Rear Admiral von Reuter used the light cruiser *Emden* as his flagship. The battleship, SMS *Bayern* can be seen in the background on Scapa Flow. Only von Reuter was allowed to use the Admiral's pinnace.

48. *Ab März 1919 nutzte Konteradmiral von Reuter den kleinen Kreuzer SMS Emden als Flaggschiff. Das Schlachtschiff SMS Bayern ist im Hintergrund in Scapa Flow zu sehen. Nur von Reuter durfte die Admiralspinasse benutzen.*

49

50. SMS *Bayern* coming into Scapa Flow passing through the anti-submarine barrier at Hoxa, 27 Nov 1918. **51/52.** British armed drifters constantly patrolled the Flow.

50. *SMS Bayern passiert die U-Boot-Sperre bei Hoxa, Scapa Flow, 27. November 1918.* **51/52.** *Britische bewaffnete Drifter patrouillierten ständig im Flow.*

53 **54**

54. German destroyers anchored at their buoys in pairs.

54. *Deutsche Zerstörer machten paarweise an den Bojen fest.*

53. A British guard destroyer (G09) anchored amongst the torpedo boats in the south-west of the Flow in Gutter Sound.

53. *Ein britische Wachzerstörer (G09) ankert nahe der Torpedoboote im Südwesten des Flow im Gutter Sound.*

55. Despite the ruling against leaving their ships, the sailor on the right of the dinghy looks like he's wearing a German sailor's hat. **56.** View of the German fleet at anchor from the Houton Seaplane terminal with Rear Admiral von Reuter's flagship, SMS *Emden,* centre front. November 1918.

55. Trotz des Verbots ihre Schiffe zu verlassen, sieht es aus als ob der Matrose rechts im Beiboot eine Deutsche Matrosenmütze trägt. 56. Blick auf die deutsche Flotte vom Houton Wasserflugzeug Terminal, November 1918. SMS Emden befindet sich vorne in der Mitte.

57. The post was regularly delivered to the Flow by mail ships such as the destroyer *B.98*. **58.** A patriotic Sweetheart postcard from Germany. **59.** SMS *Regensburg* would often carry mail and passengers back and forth between Scapa and Wilhelmshaven **60.** Mail would be distributed to the ships via British drifters flying the Internment flag.

61. Passing the hours on a destroyer deck, sitting on the torpedo tubes, chatting. **62.** Fishing was a way of wasting away the hours of constant boredom.

57. *Post wurde regelmäßig mit Postschiffen an den Flow zugestellt, etwa mit dem Zerstörer B.98.* **58.** *Eine patriotische Liebespostkarte aus Deutschland.* **59.** *Auch SMS Regensburg beförderte Post und Passagiere häufig zwischen Scapa Flow und Wilhelmshaven hin und her.* **60.** *Die Post wurde über britische Drifter, die die Internierungsflagge führten, an die Schiffe verteilt.*

61. *Zeit totschlagen auf einem Zerstörerdeck: Matrozen sitzen plaudernd zwischen Torpedorohren.* **62.** *Das Fischen war eine Art, die ständige Langeweile zu vertreiben.*

63. A four-legged companion. **64.** Pigs aboard the battleship, SMS *König*.

63. *Ein vierbeiniger Begleiter.* **64.** *Schweine an Bord des Schlachtschiffs, SMS König*

65/66. Daily scenes on a German battleship at anchor. Washday *and sleeping in the sun, Prinzregent Luitpold.*

65/66. *Tägliche Szenen auf einem deutschen Linieschiff vor Anker, SMS Prinzregent Luitpold vor Anker. Waschtag und Schlafen in der Sonne.*

67. Music was a constant source of relaxation. Sunday Concert on SMS *König*. **68.** An unidentified battleship. **69.** Smaller musical gatherings took place on torpedo boats.

70. A group of actors pose beside a destroyer's torpedo tubes. **71/72.** Others watch the performance from another boat, usually moored in pairs.

67. *Musik war eine ständige Quelle der Entspannung. Sonntagskonzert auf SMS König.* **68.** *Ein unbezeichnetes Linienschiff.* **69.** *Kleinere musikalische Versammlungen fanden auf Torpedobooten statt.*

70. *Eine Gruppe Schauspieler posiert neben einem Torpedorohr eines Zerstörers.* **71/72.** *Andere beobachten die Vorführung von einem anderen Boot aus, da diese üblicherweise in Pärchen vertäut waren.*

73-76. Life above and below deck.

77/78. The crew of torpedo boat *V.82* in 1917 when she was stationed in Zeebrügge on the coast of Belgium at Flanders.

73-76. *Leben über und unter Deck.*

77/78. *Die Besatzung von Torpedoboot V.82, aufgenommen während der Stationierung in Zeebrügge, Belgien, im Jahr 1917.*

79. Crews from the *G.86* and (**80**) the *G.39* torpedo boats. Both were part of the 1st Torpedo boat Flotilla.

79. *Besatzungen der Torpedoboote G.86 und G.39 (**80**). Beide gehörten zur 1. Torpedoboot-Flottile.*

81. A crew poses for photos on their boat in 1919.
82. A second crew celebrating Easter.

81. Eine Besatzung posiert 1919 an Bord für den Fotografen. 82. Eine zweite feiert Ostern.

83

83. A crew poses with an officer on a torpedo boat.
84. The *Sierra Ventana* taking 1,000 men and 25 officers back to Germany, 3 December 1918. **85.** Luggage is searched on deck and then (**86**) taken on to a British drifter for the transfer.

83. *Torpedobootbesatzung mit Offizier.*
84. *Die Sierra Ventana brachte am 3. Dezember 1918 1.000 Matrosen und 25 Offiziere zurück nach Deutschland.* **85.** *Gepäck wurde an Deck durchsucht und dann (**86**) zum Transport zu einem britischen Drifter gebracht.*

Scapa-Flow.
Gepäck wird v. d. Abreise durch
engl. Matrosen untersucht.

Serie I Nr. 19

Scapa-Flow. Gepäck wird zur Heimreise
auf engl. Drifter gebracht.

Serie II Nr. 20

87. The battle-cruiser, SMS *Hindenburg*, starting to settle.

87. *Der Schlachtkreuzer SMS Hindenburg beginnt zu sinken.*

DER TAG. HALF A MILLION TONS OF STEEL GOES TO THE BOTTOM

Midsummer's Day, 21 June 1919, started like any other. By day's end, however, the German fleet had succeeded in scuttling 54 out of the 72 ships interned at Scapa. It was a dramatic act of self-destruction and the biggest single loss of shipping ever recorded in history.

The plan to sink the fleet slowly took shape in great secrecy. Rear Admiral von Reuter's greatest fear was possible treachery from revolutionary sailors who wanted an end to the war at all costs and saw the scuttle as a threat to peace. Four days previously, his written orders were unwittingly distributed to his officers. Ships were to watch for an innocent-looking signal - 'Paragraph eleven, Confirm' – from his own flagship, SMS *Emden*. The signal was given at 11:00. By 12:16, British shore parties were alerted by the sounds of the tolling of the ship's bell on SMS *Friedrich der Große* as she started to list. Half an hour later, another battleship, SMS *König Albert,* followed. Sailing on Scapa Flow at the same time was a group of children aboard the Admiralty supply vessel *Flying Kestrel* on a school outing. In the bubbling, seething pandemonium, they witnessed history.

Several hours before, the British had left the Flow to carry out torpedo practice. Only at 14:30, too late to make a difference, the first four destroyers came racing back. They could do little to stop the inevitable – every measure had been taken to prevent them from doing so although the British did manage to tow a few ships on to the shores, mostly destroyers, the battleship SMS *Baden* and some light cruisers including Rear Admiral von Reuter's own, the *Emden*. What the Royal Navy had failed to accomplish when the two great fleets clashed at Jutland in 1916 – the destruction of the German fleet – the Germans had obligingly succeeded in doing in mere hours.

Life on Scapa Flow, aboard the interned ships, ended but now, classified as prisoners of war, the sailors started another seven months of captivity ashore. For their commander, von Reuter, it was worse. He faced the threat of being tried as a war criminal. At the end of January 1920, fourteen months after they had left Germany, they came home.

Nine German sailors remained. Shot by the British in the confusion of the day, they lie buried in a graveyard overlooking the Flow on Hoy, the last fatalities of the First World War.

For the British, the sinking had solved a major problem. The French had wanted to receive some of the German ships for their navy as compensation. That was no longer possible. Relations had become so strained that some French newspapers even accused the British of having known about the scuttle plans and doing nothing to prevent it so as not to give the French their share of ships.

SCAPA
1919 + 100 YEARS

DER TAG. EINE HALBE MILLION TONNEN STAHL GEHT UNTER

Mittsommertag, der 21. Juni 1919, begann wie jeder andere Tag. Doch am Ende des Tages war es der deutschen Flotte gelungen, 54 der 72 in Scapa internierten Schiffe zu versenken. Es war ein dramatischer Akt der Selbstzerstörung und der größte verzeichnete Schiffsverlust der Geschichte.

Der Plan, die Flotte zu versenken, hatte langsam unter großer Geheimhaltung Gestalt angenommen, da von Konteradmiral von Reuters größte Sorge dem Verrat revolutionärer Matrosen galt, die um jeden Preis ein Ende des Krieges wollten und die Versenkung als Bedrohung des Friedens sahen. Erst vier Tage zuvor waren seine schriftlichen Anordnungen unbeabsichtigt an seine Offiziere verteilt worden. Ein unschuldig aussehendes Signal des Flaggschiffs Emden – „Paragraph elf, Bestätigen" – sollte das Ereignis auslösen. Um 11:00 Uhr wurde es gegeben. Um 12:16 alarmierte der Klang der Schiffsglocke der sich auf die Seite legenden Friedrich der Große die britischen Küstenschiffe. Eine halbe Stunde später folgte ein weiteres Schlachtschiff, König Albert. Nur eine Gruppe von Kindern, die an Bord des Admiralitätsversorgungsschiff Flying Kestrel einen Schulausflug machte, wurde Augenzeuge des brodelnden Chaos.

Denn enige Stunden vorher hatten die Briten den Flow verlassen, um eine Torpedoübung durchzuführen. Erst um 14:30 trafen die ersten vier der zurückeilenden Zerstörer ein: zu spät, um etwas auszurichten. Sie konnten wenig tun, um das Unvermeidliche aufzuhalten. Die deutschen Matrosen hatten alles getan, um die Rettung der Schiffe zu erschweren. Dennoch gelang es den Briten, einige Schiffe an die Küste zu schleppen, meist Zerstörer, das Schlachtschiff SMS Baden und einige leichte Kreuzer, darunter auch von Reuters Flaggschiff, die Emden.

Was die Royal Navy nicht geschafft hatte, als die beiden großen Flotten 1916 vor dem Skagerrak zusammenstießen - die Zerstörung der deutschen Flotte - war den Deutschen in wenigen Stunden unwiederbringlich gelungen.

Das Leben am Flow an Bord der internierten Schiffe endete. Für die Besatzungen folgten nun weitere sieben Monate in Gefangenschaft an Land, eingestuft als Kriegsgefangene. Für ihren Kommandanten von Reuter war es schlimmer: ihm drohte eine Anklage als Kriegsverbrecher. Ende Januar 1920, vierzehn Monate nachdem sie Deutschland verlassen hatten, kamen sie nach Hause.

Neun Deutsche Matrosen blieben für immer zurück. Sie wurden in den Wirren des Tages von Briten erschossen und liegen auf einem Friedhof mit Blick auf den Fluss Hoy. Es sind die letzten Todesopfer des Ersten Weltkrieges.

Die Selbstversenkung löste ein gravierendes Problem der Briten. Denn die Franzosen hatten einige der deutschen Schiffe für ihre Marine als Reparationen gefordert. Diese Forderung war nunmehr hinfällig. Dies belastete die Beziehungen beider Stadten so sehr, dass einige französische Zeitungen die Briten beschuldigten, von den Selbstversenkungsabsichten gewusst und absichtsvoll nichts unternommen zu haben, um den Franzosen ihren Teil der Flotte vorzuenthalten.

SCAPA
1919 + 100 YEARS

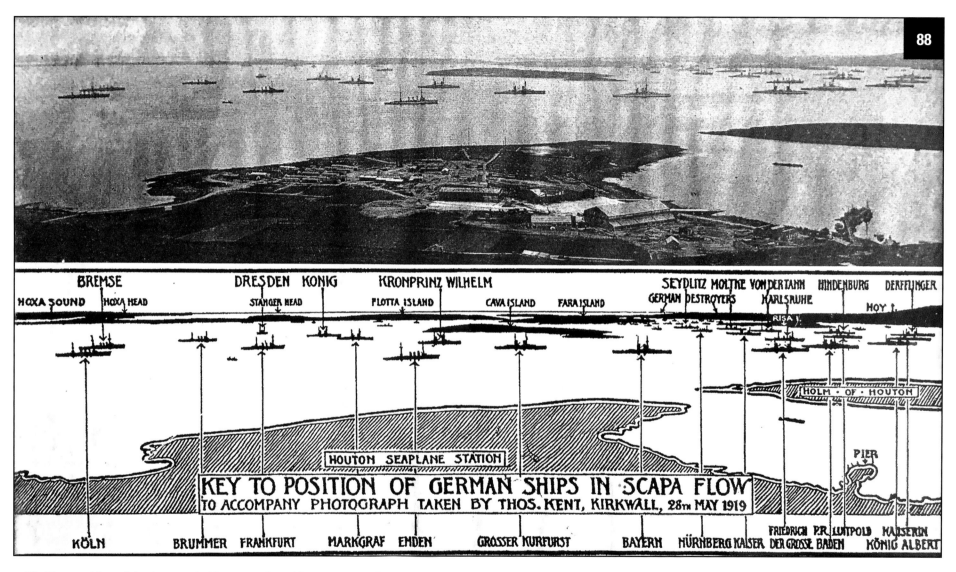

88. The position of the interned ships seen from Houton in the Flow on 28 May 1919.

88. *Die Position der internierten Deutschen Flotte am 28. Mai 1919 von Houton aus gesehen.*

89. Rear Admiral von Reuter sent the scuttle signal from his flagship, the second *Emden*, after he had moved from *Friedrich der Große*. **90.** The ship had earned the Iron Cross in 1914. Ironically, SMS *Emden* was one of the three light cruisers that was not successfully scuttled.

89. *Konteradmiral von Reuter schickte das Versenkungssignal von seinem Flaggschiff, der zweiten Emden, auf die er von Friedrich der Große gezogen war. **90.** Das Schiff hatte 1914 das Eiserne Kreuz erhalten. Ironischerweise war Emden einer der drei leichten Kreuzer, die nicht erfolgreich versenkt wurden.*

| 12:16 |

91

92

Flottenflagschiff Fried.d.Große u.Baden in Scapa-Flow.

91/92. At 12:16, a bell was heard tolling as the former flagship, SMS *Friedrich der Große*, started to list. The battleship, a veteran of the Battle of Jutland, was sinking.

91/92. Um *12:16 Uhr ertönte eine Glocke als Friedrich der Große, das ehemalige Flaggschiff, Schlagseite bekommt. Das Schlachtschiff, ein Veteran der Skaggerakschlacht, sank.*

12:45 KÖNIG ALBERT

93/94. Half an hour later, another battleship, SMS *König Albert* also sank.

93/94. *Eine halbe Stunde später sank noch ein anderes Schlachtschiff, SMS König Albert.*

Peggy Gibson

Kitty Tait

James Robertson

95. A group of around 300 schoolchildren, out on a tour of the ships, were the first witnesses amongst the sinking ships. From the *Flying Kestrel*, they had a grandstand view.

95. *Etwa 300 Kinder, die sich mit einem Schiff auf einem Schulausflug befanden, waren die ersten Zeugen der Selbstversenkung. Vom der Flying Kestrel aus hatten sie einen großartigen Blick.*

13:10 | MOLTKE

96. Five minutes later, the battle-cruiser *Moltke*, another Jutland veteran, joined the two other battleships and sank to the seabed.

97. Then, at 13:15, *Kronprinz Wilhelm*.

96. *Fünf Minuten später schloss sich der Schlachtkreuzer Moltke, ein weiterer Skagerrak Veteran, den zwei Schlachtschiffen an.*

97. *Danach, um 13:15, sank Kronprinz Wilhelm.*

97

13:25 KAISER

98. At 13:25, *Kaiser,* another veteran from the Battle of Jutland, slowly sank to the depths.

99. Photographed from the destroyer HMS *Westcott,* probably a *Kaiser* class ship is seen sinking.

98. *Um 13:25, sank Kaiser, ein weiterer Skagerrak Veteran.*

99. *Ein sinkendes Schiff der Kaiser-Klasse, aufgenommen vom Zerstörer HMS Westcott.*

13:25 GROßER KURFÜRST

100/101. Around 13:30, three ships sank: battleships SMS *Große Kurfürst* and SMS *Prinzregent Luitpold* (**103**) and the light cruiser, SMS *Dresden* (**102**).

100/101. *Um ungefähr 13.30 Uhr sanken drei Schiffe: die Linienschiffe SMS Großer Kurfürst und SMS Prinzregent Luitpold (**103**) und der Kleine Kreuzer Dresden (**102**).*

102

103

104-106. Five minutes later, the light cruiser SMS *Brummer* sank. She and SMS *Bremse* had been equipped as fast minelayers.

104-106. Fünf Minuten später, sank der Kleine Kreuzer Brummer. Er und sein Schwesterschiff, Bremse, waren als schnelle Minenleger ausgerüstet.

108

107. At 13:40 the light cruiser SMS *Köln* started to roll on to her side. Her stern was already under water ten minutes before.

108. At 13:50, the battle-cruiser SMS *Seydlitz* was added to the increasing list of scuttled ships.

107. Um 13:40 Uhr beginnt der Kleine Kreuzer SMS Köln sich langsam auf die Seite zu legen. Bereits zehn Minuten vorher war sein Heck versunken.

108. Um 13:50 Uhr sank der Schlachtkreuzer Seydlitz.

13:50 SEYDLITZ

109. SMS *Seydlitz* lying on her starboard side. Seven years later, in 1926, during the General Strike, the valuable coal in her bunkers would be used for further salvage operations to recover German vessels.

109. *Seydlitz liegt auf der Steuerbordseite. Sieben Jahre später, während des Generalstreiks 1926, wurde die wertvolle Kohle in ihren Bunkern für die Bergungsarbeiten verwendet.*

110

110. Two more battleships, *Kaiserin* and (**112/113**) *König* sank. **111.** Like *Seydlitz*, *König* lies on her side before finally sinking. She still rests on the seabed of Scapa Flow.

110. *Zwei weitere Linieschiffe, Kaiserin und (**112/113**) König sind gesunken.* **111.** *König lag wie Seydlitz, auf ihrer Seite und sank schließlich. Sie liegt immer noch im Flow.*

114. The crew of the *Nürnberg* were unsuccessful in scuttling her. She is seen here being towed to beaching.

114. *Nürnberg mislang die Selbstversenkung. Es ist zu sehen, wie sie an den Strand geschleppt wird.*

115. A British *V*-class destroyer (F 09), HMS *Vega*, seen here attempting to beach a German ship in a desperate attempt to restore order.

116-118. C.W.Burrows' photographs of *Bayern*'s sinking include time notations – (**117**) 14:00, (**118**) 14:09.

---

115. *Die Abbildung zeigt den britischen V-class Zerstörer (F 09), HMS Vega, bei dem verzweifelten Versuch ein deutsches Schiff an Land zu schleppen, um die Ordnung wieder herzustellen.*

116-118. *C.W.Burrows Fotografien von Bayerns Untergang mit Zeitangaben - (117) 14:00, (118) 14:09.*

116

118

117

119

119. SMS *von der Tann seen here at her* speed trials. At 14:15, she was scuttled.

120/122. SMS *von der Tann's* fore battery and (**121**) distinctively ventilated funnel.

119. *SMS Von der Tann, aufgenommen bei Geschwindigkeitstests. Um 14:15 Uhr wurde sie versenkt.*

120/122. *Die Vordere Batterie von SMS von der Tann und (**121**) der Schornstein mit offener Lüftung.*

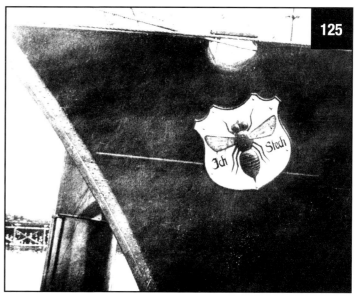

123/125. At 14:30, after having been successfully beached in Swanbister Bay, SMS *Bremse* suddenly rolled over (**123**).

*123/125. Um 14:30 Uhr, nachdem sie bereits erfolgreich in Swanbister Bay auf Strand gesetzt worden war, kenntert Bremse plötzlich (**123**).*

126

126/127. *Derfflinger,* nicknamed *The Iron Dog* by the British because she was able to take so much punishment at the Battle of Jutland (May 31 1916). **128.** At 14:45 she finally rolled and sank.

126/127. *SMS Derfflinger wurde von den Briten scherzhaft The Iron Dog (Der Eisener Hund) genannt, weil sie in der Skagerrakschlacht so viel hatte hinnehmen können.* **128.** *Erst gegen 14.45 kenterte sie und sank.*

15:00 | **KARLSRUHE**

15:45

15:50

129. An extraordinary time-series of photos taken from Houton showing the light cruiser, *Karlsruhe* (centre), gradually going down. She still rests at the bottom of the Flow.

130. Another rare time-series of photos showing the battleship, SMS *Markgraf* (**131**) gradually going down. The wreck also still remains in the Flow.

129. *Eine außergewöhnliche Fotoserie, die von Houton aufgenommen wurde und die den sinkenden leichten Kreuzer Karlsruhe (Mitte) zeigt. Sie ruht immer noch unten im Flow.*

130. *Eine weitere seltene Fotoserie, die das Linieschiff Markgraf (**131**), zeigt. Auch dieses Wrack liegt noch im Flow.*

Four stages in the sinking of the German Battleship Markgraf in Scapa Flow on June 21st 1919

J. Omond M.I.

16:45 | MARKGRAF

131

132.

132. The relatively new battle-cruiser, SMS *Hindenburg,* going down by the bow and then rolled to one side (**133**), she would end with her funnels and guns above water (**134**).

132. *Der relativ neue Schlachtkreuzer Hindenburg mit dem Bug zu sinken begann und dann zur Seite rollte (**133**) sollte er mit den Schornsteinen und Türmen aus dem Wasser ragend zu liegen kommen (**134**).*

133

135

136

137. *Baden* was the only battleship the British saved from sinking. She was beached around five o'clock.

137. *Baden war das einzige Schlachtschiff, dessen Untergang die Briten verhindert hatten. Sie wurde gegen fünf Uhr auf Strand gesetzt.*

135. The light cruiser *Nürnberg* was finally beached on Cava island. **136.** *Frankfurt* is still afloat, down in the stern.

135. *Der kleine Kreuzer Nürnberg strandete schließlich auf der Insel Cava.* **136.** *Die noch schwimmende Frankfurt mit bereits versunkenem Heck.*

137

138. Detail of *Baden*'s stern deck and a view (**139**) of *Baden* with the battleship, *König Albert* and the battle-cruiser, *Derfflinger* at anchor in Scapa Flow.

138. *Detail des Achterdecks von Baden und Blick (**139**) auf sie mit dem Schlachtschiff König Albert und dem Schlachtkreuzer Derfflinger vor Anker in Scapa Flow*

140. The German destroyers were mostly in Gutter Sound, moored in pairs at their buoys. **141**. *G.82* and *G.92* lie beached near Lyness.

---

140. *Die Zerstörer waren größtenteils paarweise in Gutter Sound festgemacht.* **141.** *G.82 und G.92 liegen am Strand in der Nähe von Lyness*

142. A German destroyer lying half submerged after the scuttle, possibly the *B.111* which had just received a fresh coat of paint on half her side.

143. Armed British marines pull alongside a German destroyer. The closest marine is carrying a Japanese Arisaka rifle.

142. Ein nach der Selbstversenkung halbversunkener deutscher Zerstörer, wahrscheinlich B.111 (die Hälfte ihrer Seite war frisch gestrichen).

143. Bewaffnete britische Marines neben einem deutschen Zerstörer. Der vordere Marine hält ein japanisches Arisaka-Gewehr.

144. A British officer climbs on to the *G.102* to hoist a British Ensign. The vessel finally came to rest in Mill Bay.

145. A painting by Bernard Gribble of Rear Admiral von Reuter's surrender. Presented by the artist to Admiral Fremantle, the British C-in-C of the 1ˢᵗ Battle Squadron.

144. *Ein britischer Offizier erklimmt G.102, um die britische Flagge zu hissen. Sie endete schließlich in Mill Bay.*

145. *Ein Gemälde der Kapitulations Konteradmiral von Reuters. Vom Künstler Bernard Gribble Admiral Fremantle (Befehlshaber des ersten Schlachtgeschwaders) zugeeignet.*

Crew of a German Destroyer taking to the boats, 21·0·1919

146. Leaving a sinking destroyer. **147.** Sailors, arms raised in surrender, arriving on shore after leaving the *Nürnberg*.

148. German officers and crew taken under tow and brought to British ships.

146. *Ein sinkender Zerstörer wird verlassen.* **147.** *Matrosen betreten das Ufer nach dem Verlassen der Nürnberg mit erhobenen Armen.*

148. *Festgenommene deutsche Offiziere und Besatzung werden auf britische Schiffe gebracht.*

149. German officers aboard a British battleship after the scuttle. **150.** Rear Admiral von Reuter on HMS *Revenge* with one of his officers.

149. Deutsche Offiziere an Bord eines britischen Schlachtschiffes nach der Selbsversenkung. 150. Konteradmiral von Reuter mit einem seiner Offiziere an Bord von HMS Revenge.

151. After being interned for 7 months, German sailors now became prisoners of war for a further 7 months in Wales. **152.** A group from *Bayern*. **153.** A mixed-ship group.

151. *Nachdem die deutschen Matrosen sieben Monate interniert worden waren, wurden sie für weitere sieben Monate zu Kriegsgefangenen.* **152.** *Eine Gruppe der Bayern.* **153.** *Eine gemischte Schiffsgruppe.*

154. The crew from *Bayern* pose for a Christmas photo, December 1919. **155.** A group of sailors pose with their British captor, Park Hall Hospital, 1920. **156.** *Derfflinger* crew members.

157-160. After their arrival in Scapa in November, the crews were steadily reduced and returned to Germany. One of the first transports, the *Graf Waldersee* (**169**) took back 150 officers and 1,000 ranks to Germany on 3 December. 2,700 men left Scapa Flow on 18 June, three days before the scuttle.

154. Weihnachtsfoto der Bayern-Besatzung, 1919. 155. Eine Gruppe von Matrosen posiert mit einem ihrer britischen Bewacher, Park Hall Hospital, 1920. 156. Besatzung der Derfflinger.

157-160. Nach der Ankunft im November wurden die Besatzungen stetig reduziert und kehrten nach Deutschland zurück. Einer der ersten Transporter, die Graf Waldersee (169), brachte am 3. Dezember 150 Offiziere und 1.000 Matrosen zurück. 2.700 Männer verließen Scapa Flow am 18. Juni, drei Tage vor der Selbstversenkung.

157

159

158

160

Scapa-Flow Leute verlassen
Dpfr. Schleswig.

161-163. The Scapa Flow sailors arrive back home in Wilhelmshaven on 31 January 1920.

161-163. Die Scapa-Besatzungen kommen am 31. Januar 1920 in Wilhelmshaven an.

164. The returning sailors are welcomed back to Germany by Admiral von Trotha (seen saluting on the extreme right) on January 31 1920. It was von Trotha who probably gave Rear Admiral Reuter his verbal orders to scuttle although this was always denied by Reuter.

164. *Die zurückkehrenden Matrosen werden am 31. Januar 1920 von Admiral von Trotha (salutierend) in Deutschland begrüßt. Wahrscheinlich hat Admiral von Trotha Konteradmiral von Reuter mündlich den Befehl zur Selbstversenkung gegeben, obwohl Reuter dies immer bestritt.*

THE GREATEST SALVAGE OF ALL TIME

Altogether, around 470,000 tons of steel had gone down to the bottom of Scapa Flow and it soon became clear that the ships needed to be salvaged, moved or destroyed. The wrecks were a hazard at low tide but their scrap value was also immense if salvage was possible.

It took 17 years to raise what had been sunk in a little under three hours, J.W.Robertson was the first man to try, raising a number of smaller destroyers employing large balloons to help lift them. But it was really Ernest Cox, a man with no previous experience in salvage, who can be called the founder of the new industry. For £24,000, he purchased the salvage rights for twenty-six destroyers and the two battle-cruisers, *Seydlitz* and the 26,180-ton *Hindenburg*.

Success only came through innovation, persistence and hard work under the most challenging conditions. With the smaller destroyers, Cox used the ebb and flow of the tides and a specially converted German dry dock with rows of powerful winches to lift the ships. For the larger ships new techniques had to be invented. Divers worked inside the hulls in the cold and dark until patches could be applied to the holes, the water pumped out and the great ships skilfully raised. In the early 1930s, another salver and a very successful businessman, Robert McCrone, carried on where Cox had left off and raised just over half the available scrap tonnage. A Glaswegian engineer and naval salvage expert, Tom McKenzie, brought his skills and focus to both, working with Cox and then McCrone in turn.

165. The salvage men of the Cox and Danks company.

165. Die Arbeiter von der Firma Cox und Danks.

DER GRÖßTE BERGUNG ALLER ZEITEN

Insgesamt waren rund 470.000 Tonnen Stahl versenkt worden, und es wurde bald deutlich, dass die Schiffe gehoben, weggeräumt oder zerstört werden mussten. Nicht nur, weil die Wracks bei Ebbe eine Gefahr darstellen, sondern auch wegen ihrem erheblichem Schrottwert im Falle einer Bergung.

Es dauerte 17 Jahre um zu heben, was in weniger als drei Stunden gesunken war. J. W. Robertson war der erste Mann, der es versuchte, indem er mehrere kleinere Zerstörer mit großen Auftriebsballons zu heben versuchte. Führend in der Branche jedoch wurde Ernest Cox, ein Mann ohne bisherige Erfahrung im Bergungsgeschäft. Für 24.000 Pfund kaufte er die Bergungsrechte von sechsundzwanzig Zerstörern und den beiden Schlachtschiffen Seydlitz, und der 26.180 Tonnen schweren Hindenburg.

Innovation, Ausdauer und harte Arbeit brachten unter schwierigsten Bedingungen den Erfolg. Bei den kleineren Zerstörern nützte Cox die Kraft der Gezeiten und ein speziell umgebautes deutsches Trockendock mit reihen von mächtigen Winden, um die Schiffe anzuheben. Für die größeren Schiffe mussten neue Techniken erfunden werden. Taucher arbeiteten in Kälte und Dunkelheit in den Rümpfen, bis die Löcher gestopft waren. Dann wurde das Wasser abgepumpt so das die großen Schiffe geschickt angehoben werden konnten. In den frühen Dreißiger Jahren knüpfte Robert McCrone, ein weiterer und sehr erfolgreicher Geschäftsmann, an Cox Arbeiten an, und hob mehr als die Hälfte der verfügbaren Schrotttonage. Tom McKenzie, ein Ingenieur und Bergungs-Experte aus Glasgow, unterstützte beide Vorhaben von Cox und McCrone mit seinem Fachwissen.

SCAPA
1919 + 100 YEARS

166. Ernest Guelph Cox (sitting), the salvage pioneer and the founder of Cox and Danks. **167.** Engineer and salvage expert Tom McKenzie RN, who worked for both Cox and McCrone. **168.** Robert McCrone, Chairman of Metal Industries. He continued Cox's work.

166. Cox (sitzend), der Begründer von Cox and Danks. 167. Ingenieur Tom McKenzie RN, der sowohl für Cox als auch für McCrone arbeitete. 168. Robert McCrone, Vorsitzender der Metallindustrie. Er setzte die Arbeit von Cox fort.

169. Raising destroyers: Using barrage balloons (Camels) to lift the smaller craft. 170. Raising destroyers: Using the high tide to lift the vessels before bringing the wrecks Into the shallower waters off Lyness.

169. *Bergung der Zerstörer mit kleineren Ballons (sog. «Camels»).* 170. *Bergung der Zerstörer mittels der Flut, um sie in die Flachwasser von Lyness zu bringen.*

LEAVING DESTROYER ON BEACH

171/172. Cox bought a large floating dock which he divided into two parts to provide lift platforms to bring up the destroyers. Ironically, the dock was part of the additional reparations Germany had to pay following the scuttle.

171/172. *Cox kaufte ein großes Schwimmdock, das er in zwei Teile aufteilte, um mit Hebebühnen die Zerstörer zu bergen. Ironischerweise war das Dock Teil der zusätzlichen Reparationszahlungen, die Deutschland nach der Selbstversenkung leisten musste.*

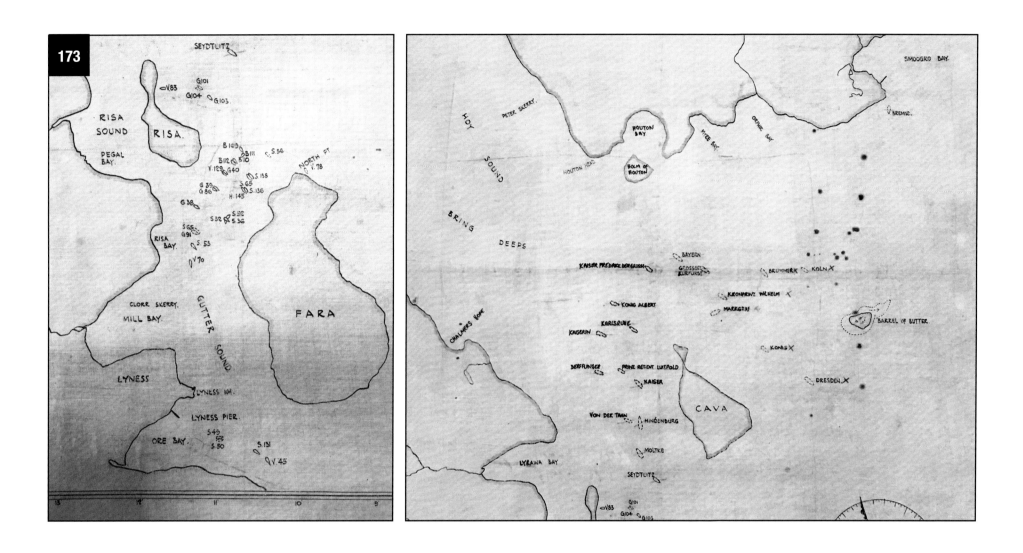

173. Map sketches of the anchorage positions made by S C George for his book *From Jutland to Junkyard*.

173. *Kartenskizzen der Ankerplätze, die S C George für sein Buch «From Jutland to Junkyard» (übers. Vom Skagerrak zum Schrottplatz) angefertigt hat.*

176. Salvage operations. Pumping and drying out SMS *Baden*.

176. Bergungsarbeiten. SMS Baden wird leergepumpt und ausgetrocknet.

174. Cox and Danks men outside the company canteen.
175. Cox and Danks divers (seen here with Cox and McKenzie). Despite the lack of contemporary regulation, Cox's safety record, though not faultless, was exemplary.

174. Cox and Danks Arbeiter von der Betriebskantine.
175. Cox and Danks Trotz der damaligen Abwesenheit von Sicherheitsstandards, war Cox's Sicherheitsbilanz, obwohl nicht ganz fehlerfrei, beispielhaft.

177. A different kind of tourism. The salvaged German vessels provided a new kind of tourist attraction to local Orcadians some of whom are pictured aboard the battleships SMS *Hindenburg*. **178.** SMS *Hindenburg* under tow.

179. *Bremse*'s rusting bow in Swanbister Bay.

177. *Eine andere Art von Tourismus. Die geborgenen Deutschen Schiffe sorgten für eine neue Art von Touristenattraktion für die Bewohner Orkneys, manche von ihnen sind an Bord des Kreuzers SMS Hindenburg zu sehen.* **178.** *SMS Hindenburg am Schlepptau.*

179. *Der rostende Bug der Bremse in Swanbister Bay.*

FORE PART OF SALVSD CRUISER BREMSE

180/181. The air-lock towers on the hull of what is probably *Kaiserin* were used by the salvers to enter different submerged compartments from the surface. They were constructed from cut-up boiler sections welded together.

182. SMS *Kaiser* on the surface, lying on her back.

180/181. *Hebung von (vermutlich) Kaiserin. Die luftdichten Schächte auf ihrem Rumpf wurden von den Bergungsunternehmen benutzt, um verschiedene Abteile betreten zu können. Sie bestanden aus verschweißten Teilen der ehemaligen Dampfkessel.*

182. *Die gehobene Kaiser, kieloben.*

Salvaging the Kaiser.

183. Ships had to be towed south across the treacherous Pentland Firth before being broken up. Pumps kept the ships stable.

184. *Moltke* being towed to the breakers.

183. *Die Schiffe mussten zum Abwracken südlich über das gefährliche Pentland Firth geschleppt werden. Sie wurden mit Pumpen stablisiert.*

184. *Moltke wird zu den Abwrackern geschleppt.*

185. HMS *Iron Duke,* Admiral Jellicoe's flagship at the Battle of Jutland, being prepared for scrap. **186/187.** *Iron Duke* listing badly after being bombed in 1939. Her hull plates were blown and she started to leak badly.

188. Cutting steel armour plate from the ships' hulls in to transportable ingots.

*185. HMS Iron Duke (Admiral Jellicoe's Flagschiff während der Sckagerrakschlacht) wird für's Abwracken vorbereitet. **186/187.** Nach einer Bombardierung hat Iron Duke 1939 schwere Schlagseite, da der Rumpf des Schiffes schwer beschädigt worden war und erheblich leckte.*

188. Die Panzerplatten werden in transportfähige Barren zerlegt.

189/190. Two views of *Derfflinger* being towed to the breakers at Faslane, 1945. She was the only ship to be towed in a floating dock.

189/190. *Zwei Ansichten von Derfflinger, die 1945 zum Abwracken nach Faslane geschleppt wurde. Sie war das einzige Schiff, das mit einem Schwimmdock geschleppt wurde.*

191. As *Derfflinger* arrives at the breakers in 1946, HMS *Iron Duke* already has had her stern removed. 192. *Derfflinger* at Scapa Flow with her new tripod foremast.

191. Als Derfflinger 1946 zum Abwracker gelangt, ist das Heck von Iron Duke bereits entfernt. 192. Derfflinger in Scapa Flow mit ihrem neuen dreibeinigem Fockmast.

WAR AND REMBRANCE

KRIEG UND ERRINERUNG

SCAPA
1919 + 100 YEARS

119

193. *Eröffnung des Marine Ehrenmals in Laboe am 30. Mai 1936, dem Vortag des Skagerraktages, in Anwesenheit der Admirale Schmidt, Behnke, von Trotha, von Bödicker, Engelhardt, von Reuter und von Levetzow. Auch Admiral Jellicoe hatte eingeladen werden sollen, war jedoch bereits im November 1935 verstorben.*

194. *1927 hatte Marinepfarrer Ronneberger, der von 1919 bis 1920 freiwillig im Internierungsverband gedient hatte, bei der Grundsteinlegung gesprochen.*

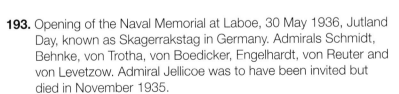

193. Opening of the Naval Memorial at Laboe, 30 May 1936, Jutland Day, known as Skagerrakstag in Germany. Admirals Schmidt, Behnke, von Trotha, von Boedicker, Engelhardt, von Reuter and von Levetzow. Admiral Jellicoe was to have been invited but died in November 1935.

194. The fleet chaplain, Pfarer Ronnenberger, who had been in Scapa Flow from 1919-1920, spoke at Laboe at the foundation stone laying in 1927.

195.

195. A life ring from SMS *Kaiserin* being handed back to the German Navy in the 1930s.

196. Father Ross with the bell from SMS *Derfflinger* on Eriskay and (**197**) that of SMS *König Albert* with Robert McCrone granddaughter, Helena.

195. *Ein Rettungsring von SMS Kaiserin wird an die deutsche Marine in den 1930er Jahren zurückgegeben.*

196. *Pater Ross mit einer der Glocken von SMS Derfflinger auf Eriskay und (**197**) der von SMS König Albert mit der Enkelin Robert McCrone, Helena.*

196

197

197/198. Germany's Commemorative medal for the scuttling. **200.** A contemporary German commemoration of the sinking.

197/198. *Eine deutsche Gedenkmedaille der Selbstversenkung.*

Alamy	115, 132, 133, 142, 148.
Author's Collection	12, 21, 37, 39, 196, 197.
Blohm und Voss, Hamburg	96, 108, 119 – 122.
Bundesarchiv, Deutschland.	6, 7, 18, 19, 20, 25, 26, 36.
Deutscher Marinebund, Laboe.	2, 5, 27, 30, 33, 34, 35, 51, 51, 53, 54, 55, 59, 60, 63, 64, 67, 69 – 76, 78 – 83, 92, 104, 105, 111, 151 – 155, 157, 160, 162, 193, 194.
Deutsches Marinemuseum, Wilhelmshaven.	8, 9, 10, 11, 13, 14, 15, 17, 22, 31, 32, 48, 49, 200.
Danish Seawar Museum, Thyborøn.	65, 66, 68, 77, 84, 89 - 91, 94, 97, 98, 101, 102, 103, 106, 107, 110, 112, 113, 115, 124, 125, 126, 127.
Family Collections	Fremantle 44, 145, Madden 43, McCrone 88, 178, 180. Reuter 45.
U.S. Library of Congress	40.
Orkney Library and Archives	50, 56, 87, 109, 114, 117, 118, 123, 128, 129, 130, 134, 135, 136, 140, 141, 143, 144, 146, 165, 166, 167, 169, 170, 173, 174, 176, 177, 179, 181, 182, 184, 185, 188, 189, 195.
Others:	Central News 29, Historianavale.com 93, Ian Buxton 168 (Metal Industries), Illustrated London News 150, Jillian Cooper 166,175, Liddle Archives, Leeds 99, Naval Ships Forum 183, Wilhelmshavener Zeitungs Bild 156, 158, 159, 161, 163, 164. Bruce Gorie 171, 172.
Public Domain	1, 23, 42, 147.

PHOTO SOURCES